OHIO

by Kathleen W. Deady

GARETH STEVENS
GS
PUBLISHING
A Member of the WRC Media Family of Companies

Please visit our web site at: **www.garethstevens.com**
For a free color catalog describing Gareth Stevens Publishing's
list of high-quality books and multimedia programs, call
1-800-542-2595 (USA) or 1-800-387-3178 (Canada).
Gareth Stevens Publishing's fax: (414) 332-3567.

Library of Congress Cataloging-in-Publication Data

Deady, Kathleen W.
    Ohio / Kathleen W. Deady.
       p. cm. — (Portraits of the states)
    Includes bibliographical references and index.
    ISBN 0-8368-4632-X (lib. bdg.)
    ISBN 0-8368-4651-6 (softcover)
    1. Ohio—Juvenile literature. I. Title. II. Series.
    F491.3.D43   2005
    977.1—dc22   2005045158

This edition first published in 2006 by
Gareth Stevens Publishing
A Member of the WRC Media Family of Companies
330 West Olive Street, Suite 100
Milwaukee, WI 53212 USA

This edition copyright © 2006 by Gareth Stevens, Inc.

Editorial direction: Mark J. Sachner
Project manager: Jonatha A. Brown
Editor: Betsy Rasmussen
Art direction and design: Tammy West
Picture research: Diane Laska-Swanke
Indexer: Walter Kronenberg
Production: Jessica Morris and Robert Kraus

Picture credits: Cover, © CORBIS; pp. 4, 11, 12, 15 © PhotoDisc; p. 5 © Corel;
p. 6 © Painet; p. 7 © North Wind Picture Archives; p. 16 © Carol Kitman; p. 22
© Chris Hondros/Getty Images; pp. 24, 26, 27 © Gibson Stock Photography;
pp. 25, 28 © Library of Congress; p. 29 © Carl Mydans/Time & Life Pictures/
Getty Images

Printed in the United States of America

1 2 3 4 5 6 7 8 9 09 08 07 06 05

CONTENTS

Chapter 1 Introduction........................4

Chapter 2 History............................6

Time Line 13

Chapter 3 People 14

Chapter 4 The Land...........................18

Chapter 5 Economy...........................22

Chapter 6 Government 24

Chapter 7 Things to See and Do 26

Glossary 30

To Find Out More.................31

Index 32

Words that are defined in the Glossary appear
in **bold** the first time they are used in the text.

On the Cover: Ohio's second largest city, Cleveland, sparkles at night.

Introduction

Ohio is a big state on the shores of Lake Erie. It has many natural wonders. These include lakes, rivers, forests, and hills.

The state's farmlands produce animals and crops. Its cities provide jobs and fun things to do. Ohio is home to the Professional Football Hall of Fame and the Rock and Roll Hall of Fame.

Ohio is also a mixture of cultures. Many well-known people have come from Ohio. They include U.S. presidents, scientists, inventors, authors, entertainers, and moviemakers.

These days, the people of Ohio make this state a great place to live and a great

Rolling farmland covers many parts of Ohio.

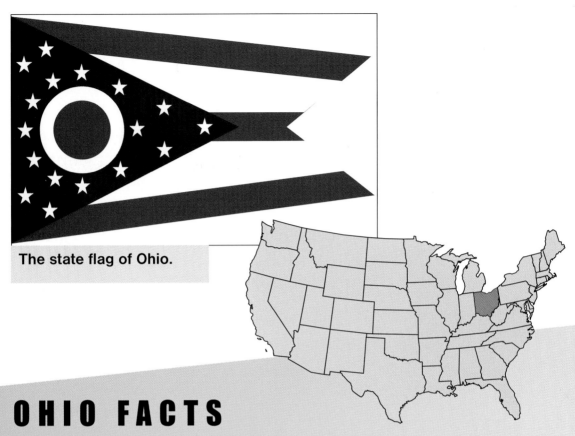

The state flag of Ohio.

OHIO FACTS

- Became the 17th state: March 1, 1803
- Population (2004): 11,459,011
- Capital: Columbus
- Biggest Cities: Columbus, Cleveland, Cincinnati, Toledo
- Size: 40,948 square miles (106,055 square kilometers)
- Nickname: The Buckeye State
- State Tree: Ohio buckeye
- State Flower: Scarlet carnation
- State Animal: White-tailed deer
- State Bird: Cardinal

History

Native Americans came to what is now the state of Ohio thousands of years ago. They hunted, following big game across the land. Later, more Natives came. They hunted in the forests and fished in the rivers and lakes. They gathered wild plants for food. Over time, they began to plant crops such as corn and squash.

Natural beauty filled Ohio when the Natives lived there. There are still some untouched places left today.

Exploration

About 1670, white men began exploring Ohio. The French came first.

In 1750, Christopher Gist from Great Britain arrived in the area. He and his men explored the land along the Ohio River. Britain had already settled some of the land to the east. They had **colonies** along the Atlantic coast. Now, they claimed the Ohio area, too.

But the French also claimed this land.

War, Land, and Freedom

In 1754, war broke out between Britain and France. Many Native people fought in this war, too. Most of the Natives sided with France. This war was called the French and Indian War. In 1763, Britain won the war. Now, Britain held most of the land east of the Mississippi River, including Ohio.

Mound Builders
Mound builders lived in Ohio for more than two thousand years. These Native Americans made big mounds of earth. They used some mounds as religious **monuments**. Other mounds became forts or burial grounds. The last group was the Mississippians. They lived in Ohio when the first Europeans came.

In the 1800s, steamboats helped improve travel and trade on the Ohio River and Lake Erie.

In 1775, another war began. This war was the Revolutionary War. The British colonies in the East had grown tired of British control. They were fighting to be free of the British. The colonies won the war in 1783. They formed their own country called the United States of America. This new country took control of the Ohio area.

IN OHIO'S HISTORY

Pontiac's War

Chief Pontiac was a Native from Ohio. He did not want the British to take his people's land. To stop them, he sided with the French in the French and Indian War. He continued to fight the British even after France and Britain signed a peace **treaty**. In 1763, he captured eight British forts. This fighting was called Pontiac's War.

Territory to Statehood

In 1787, Ohio became part of a large area of land known as the Northwest **Territory**. The next year, settlers founded Marietta. Marietta was the first town in Ohio. On March 1, 1803, Ohio became the seventeenth state of the United States of America. Chillicothe was its first capital city.

FUN FACTS

Who Was First?

The first white people in Ohio were French. Between 1669 and 1670, Robert de La Salle traveled along the Ohio River. At about the same time, Louis Jolliet explored near Lake Erie. No one knows for sure who was first.

Many more settlers came to Ohio. They took Native

land. The Natives tried to keep the settlers out. The Natives fought both the settlers and the U.S. Army. Still, the settlers kept taking more and more land. They pushed the Natives out. In 1842, the Natives were forced out of the last of their land in Ohio.

Growth and War

In the 1800s, travel became easier. Steamboats made their way along the Ohio River and Lake Erie. New roads, canals, and railroads were built. They connected Ohio to other states. Now farmers in Ohio could send their crops to markets far away.

At this time, many farmers in southern states kept black people as slaves. People in the North did not, and they wanted to outlaw slavery in the whole country. Southern states decided to form their own country. This led to the Civil War.

Famous People of Ohio

Tecumseh

Born: About 1768, Old Piqua, near modern Dayton, Ohio

Died: October 5, 1813, Chatham, Ontario, Canada

Tecumseh was a Native American. When he was young, white men killed his father. He grew up to be a powerful speaker and a great leader. In about 1810, he united many Native tribes in the eastern United States. They tried to keep the white people from taking what was left of their land. They fought the U.S. Army. They lost the fight, but Tecumseh did not give up. In the War of 1812, he sided with Britain against the Americans. He died in battle the next year.

The Underground Railroad

Slavery was legal in the South before 1865. During that time, many people in Ohio helped slaves escape from their owners in the South. They hid the slaves in barns. They helped them travel in secret. This secret system was called the Underground Railroad. It helped many slaves escape to freedom.

The Civil War began in 1861. The North and South fought each other for four years. Most people in Ohio supported the North. Finally, the North won the war, and slavery ended.

After the war, many new businesses opened in Ohio. Workers melted steel and cast it into useful products. Factories made goods from rubber and glass. Workers mined coal and iron ore. People came from far away to work in Ohio.

By the 1880s, many workers were unhappy. They worked long hours for low pay. Many factories and mines were not safe places to work. In Ohio, the workers began to fight for change. Some even refused to work until their bosses agreed to treat them fairly. These workers led the whole country in a fight for fair pay and safe working conditions.

The 1900s

In the early 1900s, Ohio was doing well. Cities grew and spread out into the nearby farmland. Then, in 1929, life changed. The **Great Depression** began in the United States. Many factories closed in Ohio. People lost their jobs and their farms. The state did not recover for many years.

Many Ohioans worked in coal mines in the 1800s. Coal mines are still providing jobs today.

The United Stated entered World War II in 1941. In Ohio, factory workers made guns, planes, ships, and tires. These jobs helped people get back to work.

Ohio Today

In the 1950s and 1960s, Ohio became a leader in space **research**. Cities such as Cleveland and Toledo became large shipping ports.

FUN FACTS

Coal Mine Fire

In 1884, coal miners in Perry County stopped working because their pay was low and the mines were unsafe. Their bosses did not listen to the miners' complaints. They did not want to change the way they ran the mines. Finally, a group of angry miners set some of the mines on fire. There was so much coal in those mines that the fires never stopped burning. They are still burning today!

Columbus is the capital city and the center of the state government.

Since then, Ohio has had problems. Businesses have closed, and people have lost their jobs once again. The air and water have often been dirty. In 1997, the Ohio River flooded many towns and caused damage. Today, Ohio is working to fix these problems.

FUN FACTS

First in Space

Two men from Ohio have led the way in space travel. In 1962, John Glenn became the first American to orbit Earth. In 1969, Neil Armstrong was the first person to step on the Moon.

★ ★ ★ Time Line ★ ★ ★

1670	The French begin exploring parts of Ohio.
1750	The British explore near the Ohio River.
1754	French and Indian War begins.
1763	Britain wins control of most of the land east of the Mississippi, including Ohio.
1787	Ohio becomes part of the Northwest Territory.
1788	U.S. settlers found Marietta, Ohio's first town.
1803	Ohio becomes the seventeenth state.
About 1810	Tecumseh unites many Native tribes in the eastern United States.
1861–1865	Many Ohioans fight for the North in the Civil War.
1929	The Great Depression begins.
1941	U.S. involvement in World War II begins.
1950s–1960s	Ohio cities become major ports on Lake Erie. Ohio becomes a leader in space research.
1997	The Ohio River floods many towns and damages them.

CHAPTER 3

People

More than eleven million people live in Ohio. Since 1990, the state's **population** has grown more slowly than that of most other U.S. states. Some businesses have left Ohio. They have moved to places where costs are lower. As a result, people have had to leave Ohio, too. They need to go where they can find work. Even so, out of all fifty states, Ohio still ranks seventh in size according to population.

Hispanics: In the 2000 U.S. Census, 1.9 percent of the people in Ohio called themselves Latino or Hispanic. Most of them or their relatives came from Spanish-speaking backgrounds. They may come from different racial backgrounds.

The People of Ohio

Total Population 11,459,011

White
85.0%

Native American
0.2%

Asian
1.2%

Other
2.1%

Black or African American
11.5%

Percentages are based on 2000 Census.

Most people in Ohio live in or near cities. Big cities such as Columbus and Cleveland have **suburbs** that spread out for many miles.

Early Population Growth

Many white people came to Ohio in the late 1700s. Some were soldiers. They fought in Ohio during the Revolutionary War. When the war ended, they stayed. Most became farmers.

In the early 1800s, the area grew fast. Many settlers came from eastern states. They wanted to farm the rich land.

Immigrants came to Ohio, too. They came from countries such as Germany and Britain. Some built canals and railroads. Others worked on farms or in factories.

During the 1840s, many Irish people moved to Ohio. The potato crop had failed in Ireland. The Irish were

Cincinnati is Ohio's third largest city.

The Amish people live as simply as they did many years ago.

Today's Ohioans

Today, the people of Ohio come from many backgrounds. Most are white. More than 10 percent of the

starving there. Some came to Ohio to start new lives.

During the late 1800s, another wave of people came. Many were African Americans who had been slaves. They did not want to stay in the South. They thought their lives might be better in Ohio and other northern states.

FUN FACTS

Designing People

In 1980, Chinese American Maya Ying Lin from Ohio designed the Vietnam Veterans Memorial, located in Washington, D.C.

people are African American. A small number of Native Americans and Asians also call Ohio home.

Many Amish people live in Ohio. The Amish do not use electric lights, cars, or telephones. They live life simply. Ohio has more Amish people than any other U.S. state.

Education and Religion

The first school opened in Ohio in 1773. Now, the state has many fine public and private schools.

Ohio has many colleges and universities. The largest is Ohio State University. Oberlin College is also well known. It was the first college in the country to serve women as well as men.

Most people in Ohio are Christians. Most of these Christians are Protestants.

A small number of Jews, Muslims, and Buddhists also make Ohio their home.

Famous People of Ohio

Thomas Edison

Born: February 11, 1847, Milan, Ohio

Died: October 18, 1931, West Orange, New Jersey

Thomas Edison was a famous inventor. When he was a boy, he became hard of hearing. Even so, he was a curious child. He wanted to know how things worked and how he could make them work better. After he grew up, he created the first useful and safe electric light bulb. He also invented the record player and the moving picture camera. He was the first person to make a movie, too. Edison invented more than one thousand new things. Many of them made people's lives easier.

The Land

The land in Ohio has changed a great deal in the past few hundred years. Long ago, hardwood forests covered most of the state. Today, cities and farms cover much of the land instead.

The southwestern part of the state still has big forests. The land there is too rough for farming. In the north part of the state, lowlands surround Lake Erie. Where this land has not been drained, it tends to be swampy.

Land in the eastern part of the state contains hills and **plateaus**. It is higher than the land to the north. Rich farmlands roll through the western part of Ohio. Campbell Hill is in this part of the state. At 1,550 feet (472 meters) above sea level, it is the highest point in Ohio.

Ohio's land also has many riches underground. The east and southeast have coal deposits. Many parts of the state have oil and natural gas reserves. Large areas contain sand, clay, and gravel. Sandstone and limestone are found in Ohio, too.

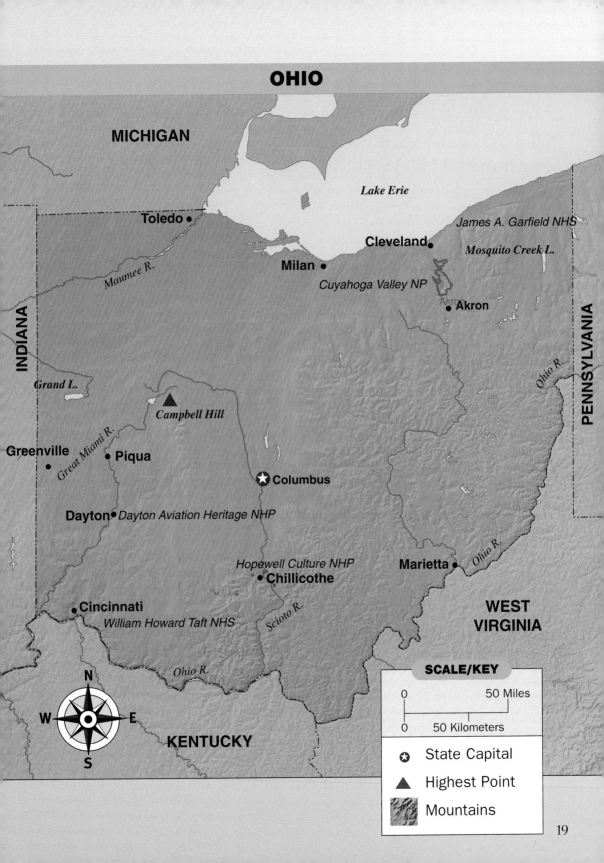

OHIO

MICHIGAN

Lake Erie

Toledo •

Cleveland •

James A. Garfield NHS

Mosquito Creek L.

Milan •

Cuyahoga Valley NP

AKRON

• Akron

INDIANA

PENNSYLVANIA

Maumee R.

Grand L.

▲
Campbell Hill

Greenville

• Piqua

Great Miami R.

☆ Columbus

Dayton • *Dayton Aviation Heritage NHP*

Ohio R.

Hopewell Culture NHP
• Chillicothe

Marietta •

Ohio R.

WEST
VIRGINIA

Cincinnati •
William Howard Taft NHS

Scioto R.

Ohio R.

KENTUCKY

N
W E
S

SCALE/KEY

0	50 Miles
0	50 Kilometers

☆ State Capital

▲ Highest Point

▦ Mountains

19

Lakes and Rivers

Ohio has more than twenty-five hundred lakes. The largest is Lake Erie. It forms the border between Ohio and Canada. Lake Erie is one of the five Great Lakes.

Ohio has many rivers, too. The longest is the Ohio River, which forms much of the state's eastern and southern borders. Most other rivers in Ohio flow

south into the Ohio. The Muskingum River and the Scioto River are among them. Some rivers in Ohio, however, flow north and empty into Lake Erie.

Major Rivers

Ohio River
975 miles (1,569 km) long

Scioto River
237 miles (381 km) long

Muskingum River
120 miles (193 km) long

FUN FACTS

The Ohio River

The Ohio River is one of the largest rivers in North America. It twists and turns along the state's southern border. Across the river are Kentucky and West Virginia. The name *Ohio* comes from an Iroquois word. It means "great water." The river gave the state its name.

Climate

Ohio's weather varies. Cold, dry air flows down from Canada in the winter months. Warm, humid air flows up from the south in the summer months.

Plants and Animals

Ohio's forests have many kinds of trees. Most are hardwood trees, such as beeches, maples, and oaks. Azaleas, dogwoods, and hawthorns are among the state's most common shrubs. Many wildflowers color Ohio in the spring and summer. They include blazing stars and lilies.

Long ago, large animals such as bison, wolves, and cougars roamed freely around the area that is today Ohio. Now, the state has few large animals left. Only white-tailed deer are still common. A small number of black bears live there, too.

Ohio has many smaller animals. Beavers build dams along streams. Raccoon and mink feed in shallow waters. Muskrat, opossums, cotton-tail rabbits, red foxes, skunks, and weasels live throughout the state.

Ohio has many birds. Wild ducks, turkeys, geese,

pheasant, and quail are among the game birds that live there. Songbirds living there include blackbirds and cardinals. The cardinal is the state bird.

Many kinds of fish swim in the lakes and rivers of Ohio. Bass, catfish, perch, bluegills, saugers, and walleyed pike all live in the state's waters.

FUN FACTS

Saving the Wood Duck

Many wood ducks live in Ohio. Yet just one hundred years ago, wood ducks were almost gone in North America. The U.S. government started a program to save them. The program worked, and the duck population grew. Today, many wood ducks live in the area again.

Economy

Years ago, most people in Ohio were farmers. Then in the late 1800s, factories grew. Workers began making goods from steel, rubber, and clay. Trains and ships carried these products to other states. Ohio became one of the great **industrial** states. Today, farming and industry still create many jobs in Ohio.

Farming and Industry

Corn, soybeans, hay, potatoes, wheat, oats, and tomatoes are all important crops in Ohio. In fact, Ohio makes more tomato juice than any other state.

A factory
worker welds
a chair in
Haskins, Ohio.

22

Some farmers raise chickens for meat and eggs. Others rear hogs or beef cattle. Dairy cattle and sheep are raised in Ohio, too. Sheep are kept for both meat and wool.

Workers in **foundries** and factories make steel, tools, car parts, rubber, electronic equipment, transportation equipment, paper, and ships.

Mining and Tourism

People in Ohio also work in mining jobs. Ohio's mines provide large amounts of crushed stone, salt, sand, gravel, and limestone.

Many people in the state work in service jobs. Some work in hotels and restaurants. Others work at sports events, museums, and state parks.

How Money Is Made in Ohio

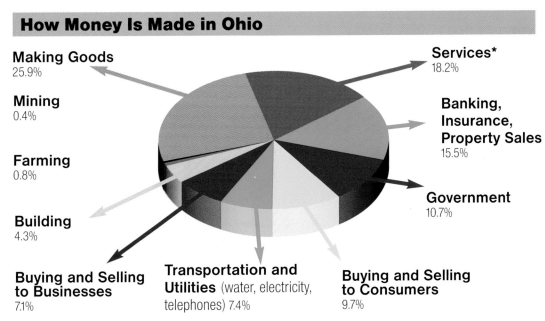

Making Goods
25.9%

Mining
0.4%

Farming
0.8%

Building
4.3%

Services*
18.2%

Banking, Insurance, Property Sales
15.5%

Government
10.7%

Buying and Selling to Businesses
7.1%

Transportation and Utilities (water, electricity, telephones) 7.4%

Buying and Selling to Consumers
9.7%

* Services include jobs in hotels, restaurants, auto repair, medicine, teaching, and entertainment.

Government

Ohio's leaders work in Columbus. Columbus is the capital city. The state government has three parts, or branches. They are the executive, legislative, and judicial branches.

Executive Branch

The executive branch makes sure the state's laws are carried out. At the head of this branch is the governor. The lieutenant governor helps the governor. A **cabinet** also helps the governor make important decisions.

Ohio leaders work at the State Capitol Building in Columbus.

Rutherford B. Hayes was one of seven men from Ohio who became president of the United States.

It is made up of two groups. One group is called the Senate, and the other group is called the House of Representatives. These two groups work together.

Judicial Branch

The judicial branch **interprets** the state's laws. This branch includes judges and courts. Judges make sure a person accused of committing a crime gets a fair trial. Courts may decide whether or not the person is guilty.

Legislative Branch

The legislative branch makes new laws and changes old laws. The state legislature is called the General Assembly.

County Governments

Ohio is divided into eighty-eight counties. A group of three people governs each county.

OHIO'S STATE GOVERNMENT

Executive		Legislative		Judicial	
Office	Length of Term	Body	Length of Term	Court	Length of Term
Governor	4 years	Senate (33 members)	4 years	Supreme (7 justices)	6 years
Lieutenant Governor	4 years	House of Representatives (99 members)	2 years	Appeals (12 courts)	6 years

CHAPTER 7

Things to See and Do

Ohio has many great things to see and do. Every August, the Ohio State Fair takes place in Columbus. It is one of the largest fairs in the country. For twelve days, people sell food and display arts and crafts. They show their farm animals, too. Some win prizes for the best animals. Almost one million people visit this fair each year.

Music, Theater, and Art

The Cleveland Orchestra is one of the best in the world. The

FUN FACTS

Rock and Roll Hall of Fame

The Rock and Roll Hall of Fame is in Cleveland. It has displays, films, and videos. They show the history of rock and roll music. Visitors can see many items that belonged to famous musicians. Some of John Lennon's school report cards and Jim Morrison's Cub Scout uniform are displayed there.

Large decorated guitars are on display at the Rock and Roll Hall of Fame and Museum.

Steven Spielberg

Born: December 18, 1947, Cincinnati, Ohio

Steven Spielberg is a famous movie director. He also writes and produces movies. He has been making movies since he was a child. In 1975, he directed the movie *Jaws*. It was about a huge great white shark. The movie was a big hit, and it made Spielberg famous. Since then, he has directed more hit movies. They include *E.T. the Extraterrestrial*, *Raiders of the Lost Ark,* and *Jurassic Park*. He has won many awards for his outstanding work in the movies.

Cincinnati Symphony Orchestra is also respected.

Ohio has great theaters, too. An outdoor theater near Chillicothe is popular in the summer. Actors perform the play *Tecumseh* at this theater. The play tells the story of this great Native leader.

Ohio cities also have many art centers. In 1878, the Columbus Museum of Art was the first art museum to open in Ohio. The Cleveland Museum of Art displays art from Europe and Asia. Some of this art is hundreds

Visitors see displays like this space capsule at the Neil Armstrong Air and Space Museum in Wapakoneta.

Famous People of Ohio

Annie Oakley

Born: August 13, 1860, Darke County, Ohio

Died: November 3, 1926, Greenville, Ohio

Annie Oakley's real name was Phoebe Ann Moses. She liked to shoot guns, even when she was young. As she grew up, she became a famous **sharpshooter**. She was very fast and always hit her target. She could shoot a playing card in half! She could shoot a dime in midair from 90 feet (27 m) away! For many years, Annie performed in Buffalo Bill's Wild West Show. She performed for people all over the United States and Europe.

Members of the first pro baseball team, the Cincinnati Red Stockings, are shown here in 1869.

of years old. The Toledo Art Museum has many kinds of glass art, and the city is known as the glass capital of the world. People visit the Akron Art Museum to see folk art, modern art, and photography.

Sports

Ohio has many big-league sports teams. Football fans cheer for the Cincinnati Bengals and the Cleveland Browns. Thousands of fans from Ohio and across the nation visit the Football Hall of Fame in Canton, too.

Baseball fans cheer for two teams as well. The Cincinnati Reds have won the World Series four times. The Cleveland Indians have won twice.

The Cleveland Cavaliers play basketball. Hockey fans go to Columbus to see the Blue Jackets play.

Kids from around the world race homemade cars in the All-American Soap Box Derby in Akron.

College football fans went wild in 2003 when the Ohio State Buckeyes won the Fiesta Bowl.

Soap-Box Derby

Every July, many people attend the All-American Soap Box Derby in Akron. This is a big car race for children. Kids ages nine to sixteen come from all over the country to compete. Some come from other countries, too. They race homemade cars without motors. These cars are called "soap boxes."

GLOSSARY

cabinet — a team of people who advise the governor

colonies — groups of people living in a new land but still controlled by the place they came from

foundries — places where metal is melted and put into molds to make various products

Great Depression — a time when many people lost jobs and businesses lost money in the 1930s

immigrants — people who come to a country from another country to live

industrial — having to do with factories and other businesses that make goods

interprets — explains the meaning of something

monuments — something built to remember someone or an event

plateaus — large, flat areas that are higher than the land around them

population — the number of people who live in a place.

research — careful study to learn something new

sharpshooter — a person who is very good at hitting the mark when shooting

suburbs — areas with a lot of people close to a city

territory — an area that belongs to a country

treaty — a written agreement

Books

B Is for Buckeye: An Ohio Alphabet. Sleeping Bear Alphabet Books (series). Marcia Schonberg (The Gale Group)

Cardinal Numbers: An Ohio Counting Book. State Counting (series). Marcia Schonberg (The Gale Group)

The Legend of Blue Jacket. Michael P. Spradin (Harper Collins)

Ohio. Seeds of a Nation (series). P. M. Boekhoff and Stuart A. Kallen (KidHaven Press)

Ohio Facts and Symbols. The States and Their Symbols (series). Emily McAuliffe (Bridgestone Books)

People of Ohio. Heinemann State Studies (series). Marcia Schonberg (Heinemann)

Web Sites

Discover Ohio Kids Stuff
www.discoverohio.com/kids/homework.asp

Enchanted Learning Ohio
www.enchantedlearning.com/usa/states/ohio

For Kids Only
www.dnr.state.oh.us/parks/kids/default.htm

The Mound Builders
www.watertown.k12.ma.us/americanhistorycentral/
01firstamericans/The_Moundbuild.html

★ ★

African Americans 9–10, 14, 16, 17
Akron 28, 29
All-American Soap Box Derby 29
Amish 16, 17
Armstrong, Neil 12, 27

baseball 28, 29
basketball 29

Campbell Hill 18
Chinese Americans 16
Cincinnati 15, 27–29
Civil War 9–10
Cleveland 11, 15, 26, 27, 29
coal and coal mining 10, 11, 18
Columbus 12, 15, 24, 26, 27, 29

Edison, Thomas 17
education 17

farming 4, 9, 15, 18, 22–23, 26
France 6–8
French and Indian War 7, 8

German Americans 15
Gist, Christopher 6

Glenn, John 12
Great Britain 6–8, 15
Great Depression 10–11

Hayes, Rutherford B. 24
Hispanics (Latinos) 14
hockey 29

Irish Americans 15–16

Jolliet, Louis 8

Lake Erie 4, 7–9, 18, 20
lakes 20
La Salle, Robert de 8
Lennon, John 26
Lin, Maya 16

Marietta 8
Morrison, Jim 26
mound builders 7
museums 27–28
music 26–27

Native Americans 6–9, 17, 20
Neil Armstrong Air and Space Museum 27

Oakley, Annie 28
Ohio River 6–9, 12, 20
Ohio State Fair 26
Ohio State University 17, 29

Perry County 11
pollution 12
Pontiac's War 8
Professional Football Hall of Fame 4, 29

religion 17
Revolutionary War 7–8, 15
rivers 20
Rock and Roll Hall of Fame and Museum 4, 26

slaves and slavery 9–10, 16
space 11, 12, 27
Spielberg, Steven 27
sports 28–29
steamboats 7, 9

Tecumseh 9, 27
Toledo 11, 28

Underground Railroad 10

Vietnam Veterns Memorial 16

War of 1812 9
wood ducks 21
workers' rights 10
World War II 11